D0847393

EGGS, LEGS, WINGS

A Butterfly Life Cycle

BY SHANNON KNUDSEN

ILLUSTRATED BY SIMON SMITH

Consultant: Laura Jesse
Plant and Insect Diagnostic Clinic
Iowa State University, Ames, Iowa

CAPSTONE PRESS
a capstone imprint

First Graphics are published by Capstone Press,
151 Good Counsel Drive, P.O. Box 669, Mankato, Minnesota 56002.
www.capstonepub.com

Books published by Capstone Press are manufactured with paper
containing at least 10 percent post-consumer waste.

Library of Congress Cataloging-in-Publication Data
Knudsen, Shannon, 1971–
 Eggs, legs, wings : a butterfly life cycle / by Shannon Knudsen; illustrated by
Simon Smith.
  p. cm. — (First graphics. Nature cycles)
 Includes bibliographical references and index.
 Summary: "In graphic novel format, text and illustrations describe the life cycle of
a monarch butterfly"—Provided by publisher.
 ISBN 978-1-4296-5367-1 (library binding)
 ISBN 978-1-4296-6228-4 (paperback)
 1. Butterflies—Life cycles—Juvenile literature. 2. Monarch butterfly—Life cycles—
Juvenile literature. I. Title.
 QL544.2.K58 2011
 595.78'9156—dc22   2010029083

Editor: **Gillia Olson**
Designer: **Lori Bye**
Art Director: **Nathan Gassman**
Production Specialist: **Eric Manske**

Printed in the United States of America in Stevens Point, Wiscsonsin.
092010   005934WZS11

Table of Contents

A Cycle of Changes

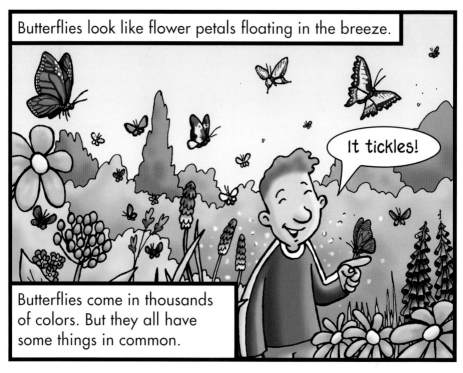

Butterflies look like flower petals floating in the breeze.

It tickles!

Butterflies come in thousands of colors. But they all have some things in common.

head

thorax

abdomen

Like all insects, they have three main body parts and six legs.

A hard exoskeleton covers their body.

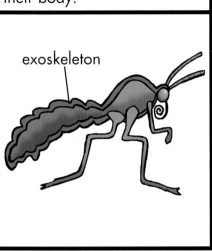

exoskeleton

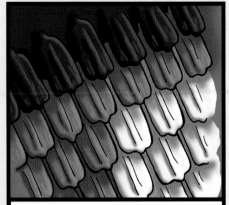

Their wing color comes from tiny scales. Monarch butterflies have bold black and orange wings.

But monarchs and other butterflies don't start their lives with wings.

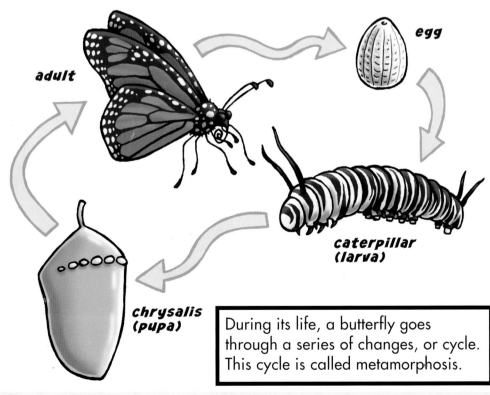

adult

egg

caterpillar (larva)

chrysalis (pupa)

During its life, a butterfly goes through a series of changes, or cycle. This cycle is called metamorphosis.

The cycle begins as a female monarch lays eggs. She puts them on milkweed plants, just one egg per leaf.

Each egg is as tiny as the head of a pin.

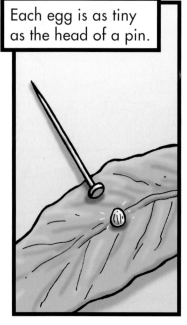

After about three days, something chews a hole from inside the egg.

The tiny creature crawls its way out.

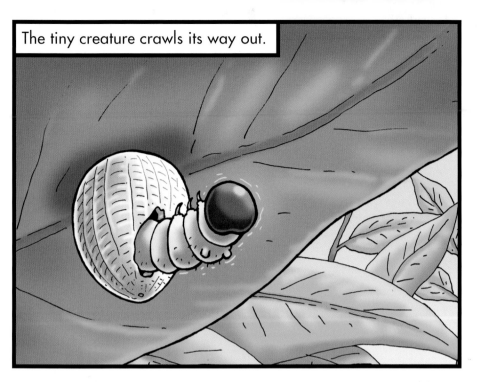

The creature looks like a worm with many little feet. It's called a caterpillar, or larva.

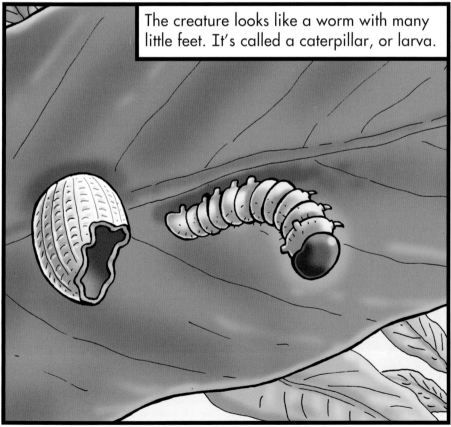

The Growing Caterpillar

A caterpillar eats and eats. Its eggshell is the first thing on the menu.

Then it eats the leaf where it was born.

The caterpillar gets stronger. It crawls to other leaves to find food.

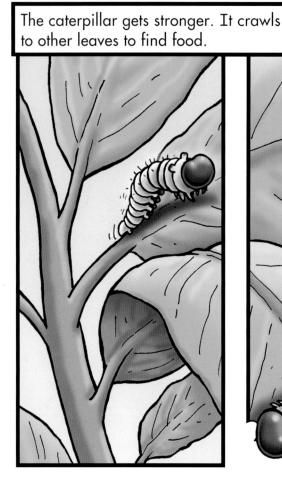

Young caterpillars face dangers. At first, they are so small that a drop of rain could wash them away.

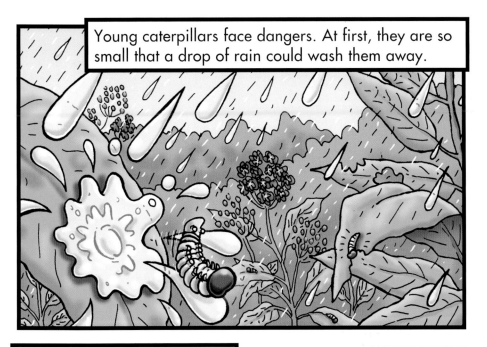

Spiders, wasps, and other bugs hunt and eat caterpillars.

Caterpillars have one defense. The milkweed they eat makes them poisonous.

Some birds and mice get sick from eating them. They know to stay away from these caterpillars.

As the caterpillar eats, it gets fatter.
Soon its skin gets too tight and splits.

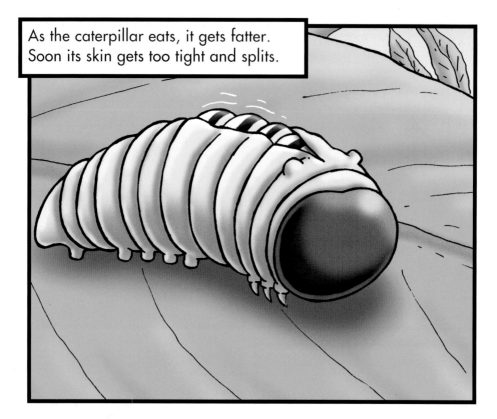

The caterpillar crawls out. A new, loose skin covers it now.

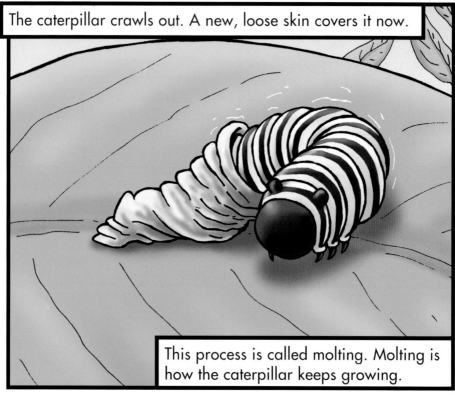

This process is called molting. Molting is
how the caterpillar keeps growing.

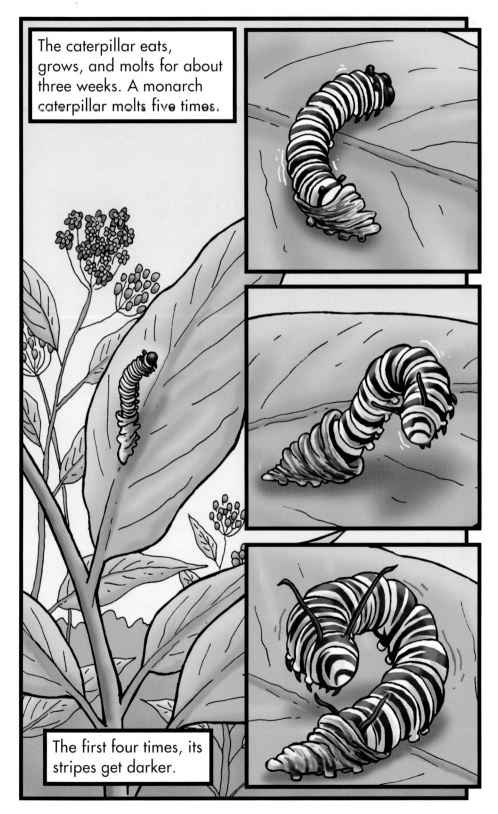

The caterpillar eats, grows, and molts for about three weeks. A monarch caterpillar molts five times.

The first four times, its stripes get darker.

11

The fifth molt is special. The caterpillar finds a branch. It spins a small pad of silk.

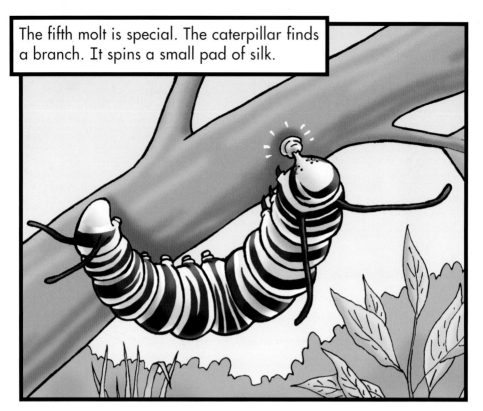

The caterpillar grabs onto the silk with tiny hooks on its feet. It hangs upside down.

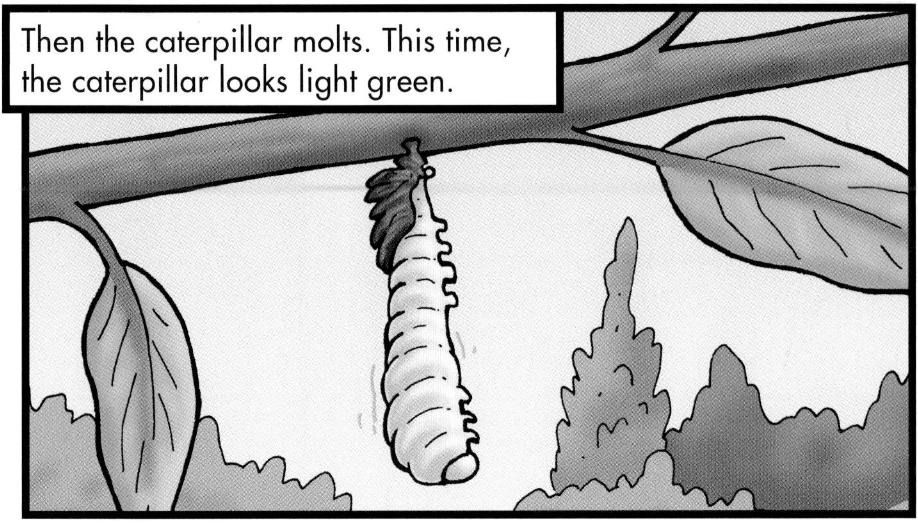
Then the caterpillar molts. This time, the caterpillar looks light green.

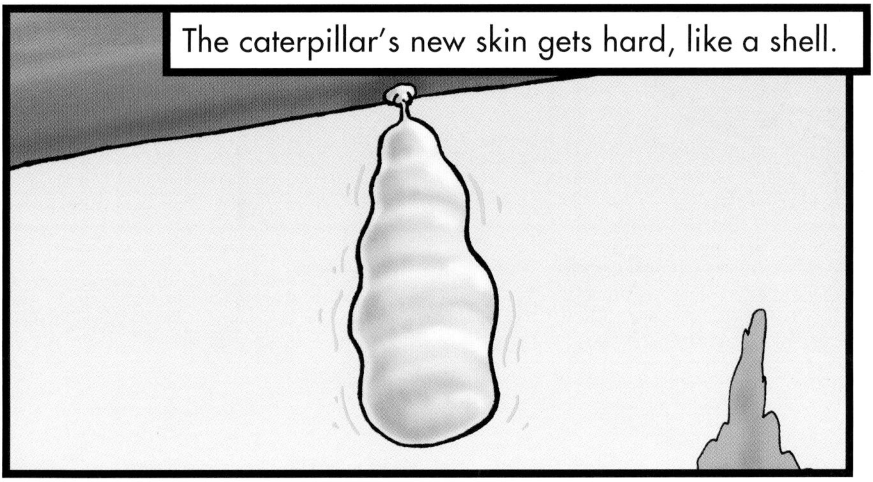
The caterpillar's new skin gets hard, like a shell.

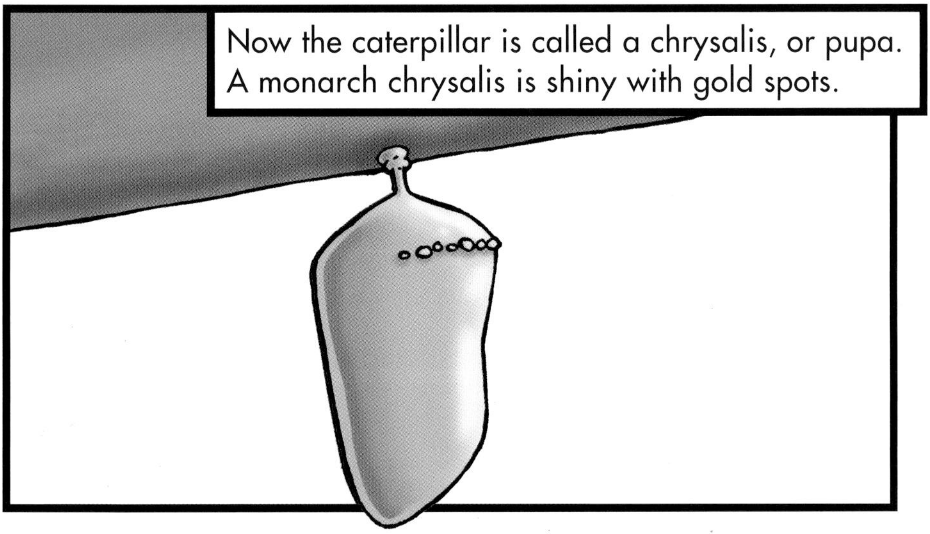
Now the caterpillar is called a chrysalis, or pupa. A monarch chrysalis is shiny with gold spots.

Inside the chrysalis, wings, legs, and other adult body parts are growing. After 10 days, the chrysalis seems to lose color.

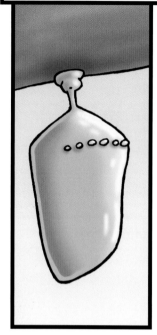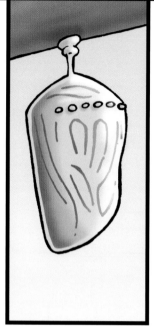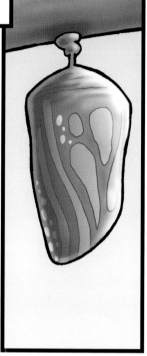

By the end, the chrysalis becomes clear. The next step is about to begin.

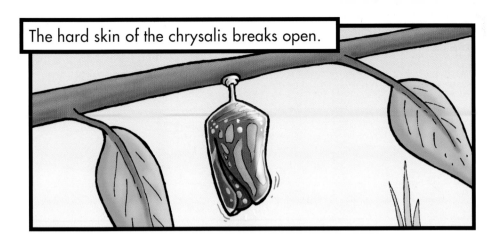

The hard skin of the chrysalis breaks open.

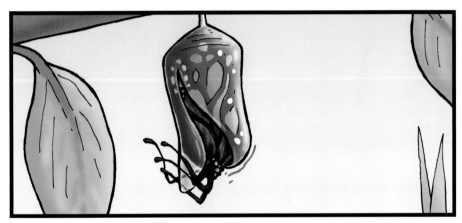

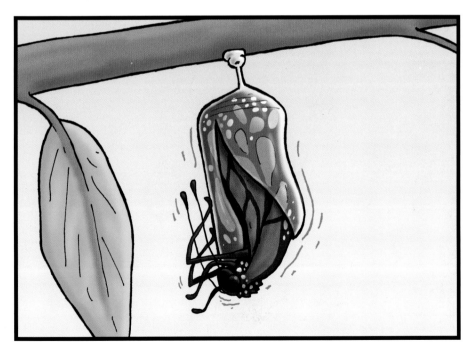

The Adult Butterfly

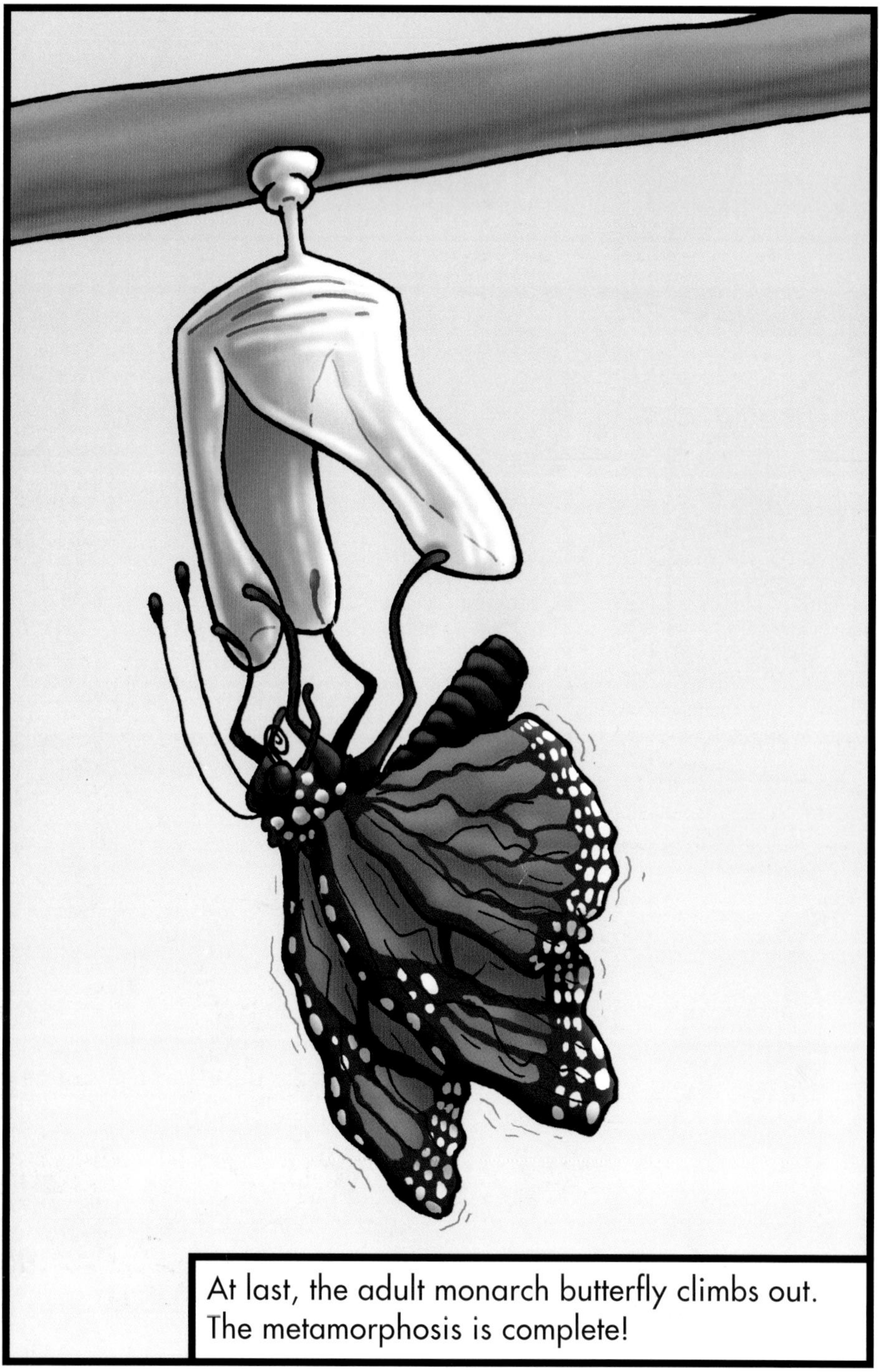
At last, the adult monarch butterfly climbs out. The metamorphosis is complete!

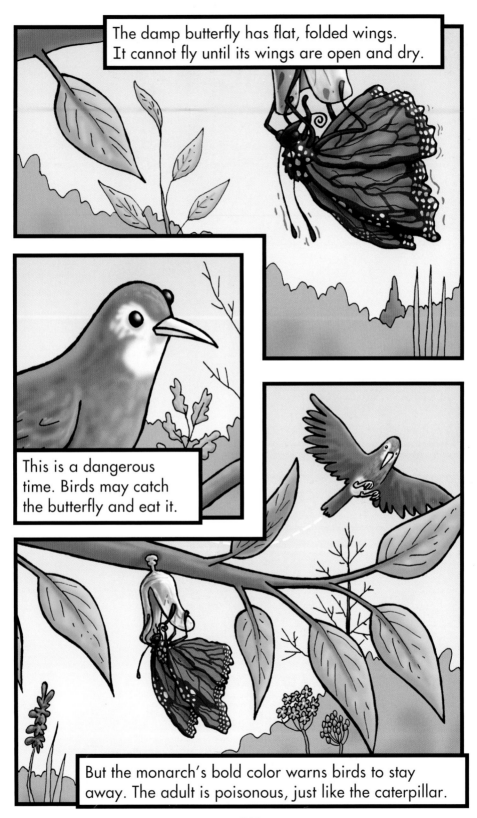

The damp butterfly has flat, folded wings. It cannot fly until its wings are open and dry.

This is a dangerous time. Birds may catch the butterfly and eat it.

But the monarch's bold color warns birds to stay away. The adult is poisonous, just like the caterpillar.

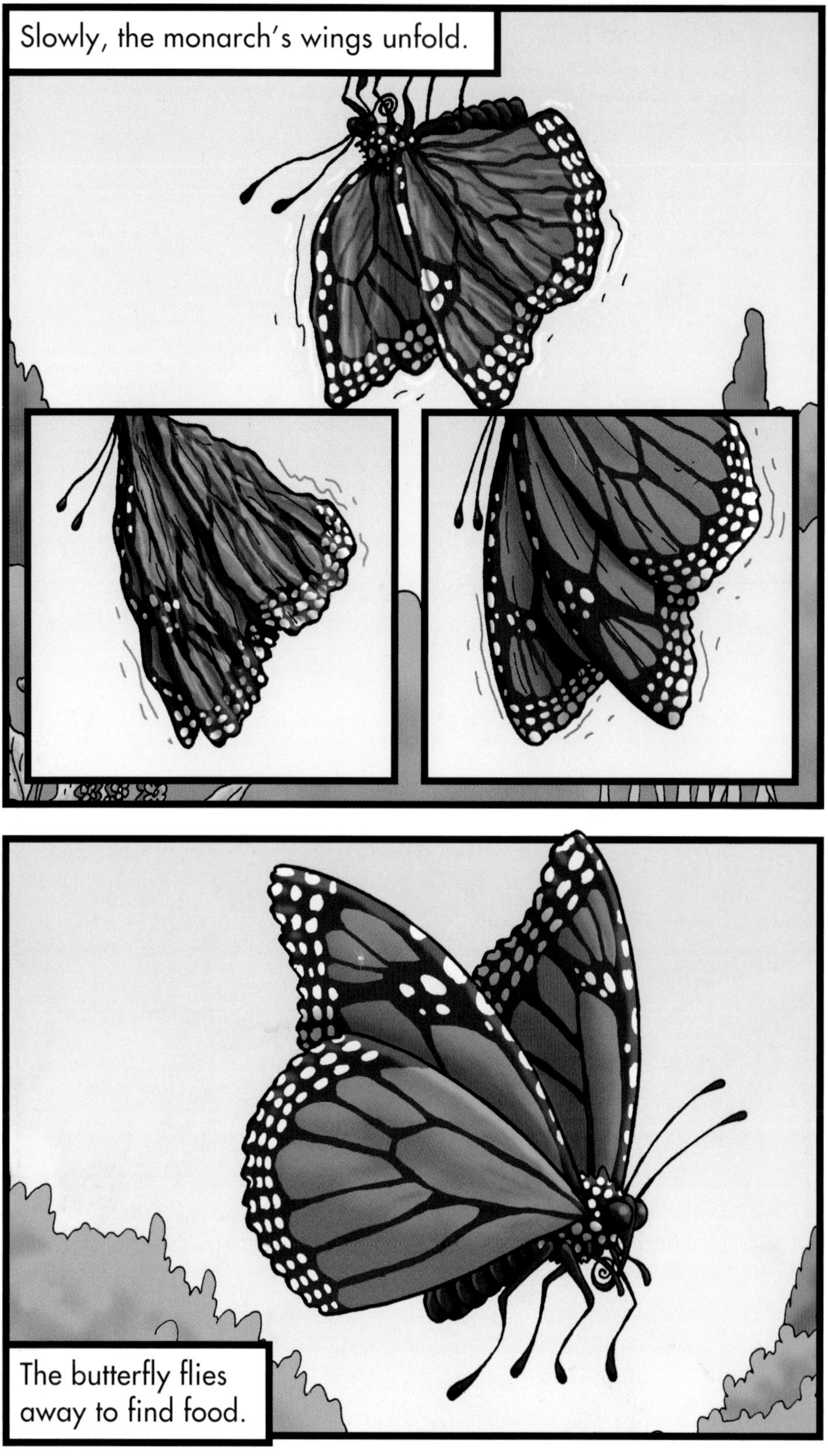
Slowly, the monarch's wings unfold.
The butterfly flies away to find food.

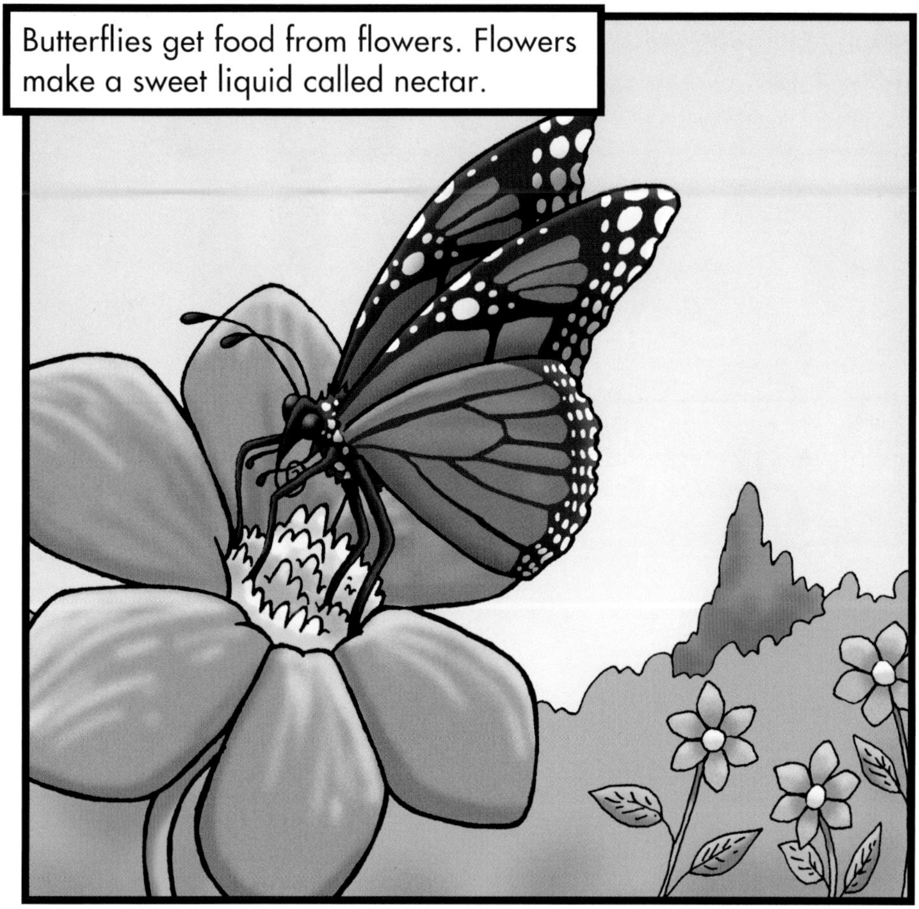
Butterflies get food from flowers. Flowers make a sweet liquid called nectar.

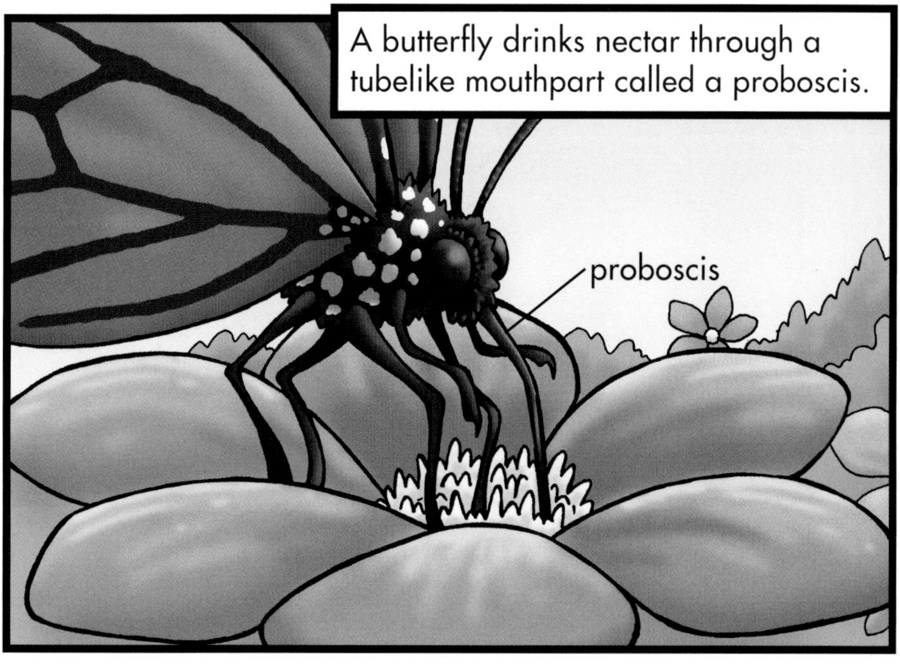
A butterfly drinks nectar through a tubelike mouthpart called a proboscis.
proboscis

Adult monarchs born in spring and summer live for a few weeks. Monarchs born in fall migrate south to escape cold weather. They live until the next spring.

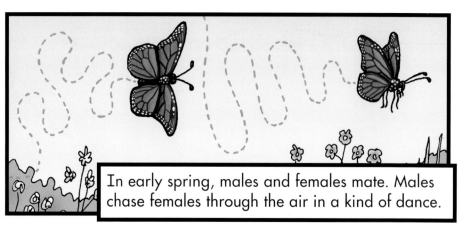

In early spring, males and females mate. Males chase females through the air in a kind of dance.

There will be more monarchs soon!

The monarchs return north in spring. The female finds a milkweed plant where she lays her eggs.

The egg begins a new life cycle.

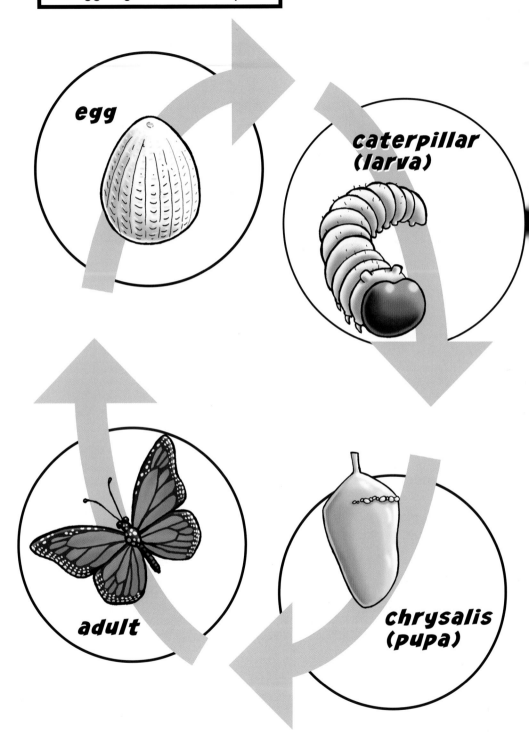

egg

caterpillar (larva)

adult

chrysalis (pupa)

Glossary

chrysalis—the third life stage of a butterfly; pupa is another word for chrysalis

exoskeleton—the hard outer shell of an insect; the exoskeleton covers and protects the insect.

larva—an insect at the stage in its life cycle between an egg and a pupa; butterfly larvae are also called caterpillars

metamorphosis—the series of changes some animals go through as they develop from eggs to adults

migrate—to move from one place to another when seasons change or when food is scarce

molt—to shed an outer layer of skin, or exoskeleton, so a new exoskeleton can be seen

nectar—a sweet liquid made by many kinds of flowers; butterflies drink nectar

proboscis—a long, tube-shaped mouthpart; a butterfly uses its proboscis to drink nectar

pupa—an insect at the stage in its life cycle between larva and adult; for butterflies, chrysalis is another word for pupa

Read More

Bishop, Nic. *Nic Bishop Butterflies and Moths.* New York: Scholastic Nonfiction, 2009.

Kalman, Bobbie. *Caterpillars to Butterflies.* It's Fun to Learn about Baby Animals. New York: Crabtree Pub. Co., 2009.

Sexton, Colleen. *The Life Cycle of a Butterfly.* Blastoff! Readers 3: Life Cycles. Minneapolis: Bellwether Media, 2010.

Slade, Suzanne. *From Caterpillar to Butterfly: Following the Life Cycle.* Amazing Science: Life Cycles. Minneapolis: Picture Window Books, 2009.

Internet Sites

FactHound offers a safe, fun way to find Internet sites related to this book. All of the sites on FactHound have been researched by our staff.

Here's all you do:

Visit *www.facthound.com*

Type in this code: 9781429653671

Check out projects, games and lots more at
www.capstonekids.com

Index

TITLES IN THIS SET:

EGGS, LEGS, WINGS
A Butterfly Life Cycle

HIDE and SEEK MOON
The Moon Phases

SEED, SPROUT, FRUIT
An Apple Tree Life Cycle

WATER GOES ROUND
The Water Cycle